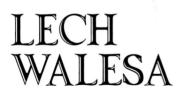

People Who Have Helped the World

LECH WALESA

by Mary Craig

For a free color catalog describing Gareth Stevens' list of high-quality children's books call 1-800-341-3569

Picture Credits
Associated Press: 7, 10, 49; Camera Press — 6-7, 21, Dirk Buwalda 22 (below left), Jan Hausbrandt 27, W. Krynski 36-37, Bob Wales 45 (top); Mary Craig: 11 (top); Dachau Museum: 5; Janina Jaworska, Warsaw: 4; Keston College: 11 (below), 57; David King: 13; Popperfoto: 54; Rex Features — cover, Laski/Setbourn 40, Laski 44, 50; Frank Spooner — Bogdan Borkowski 18 (below), 20, Mark Bulka 31, 32, 33, 34, 37, 42, Thierry Campion 45 (below), J. Czarnecki 24, 25, 43 (both), 58-59, Gamma 51, Chip Hires 55, Klahr 22 (below right), Kok 18 (top), 46 (top), 52-53, François Lochon 16-17, 19, 38, 39, 48, Remis Martin 22 (top), N.S.P./Gamma 56, Jean-Paul Paireault 28, Simon & Francolin 15, Bob Wales 41; Voice of Solidarity: 46 (below). Map drawn by Geoff Pleasance.

I would like to thank the unknown — even to me — Polish writer who was originally writing this book for us. "Josef," as we called our anonymous author, disappeared after having completed only a third of the manuscript. To this person, and the thousands of brave Polish people who have faced danger and imprisonment, I can only give my thanks and the thanks of everyone else who believes in the cause of freedom.

I would also like to thank Mary Craig, the author of *The Crystal Spirit*, the most powerful book about Lech Walesa. She took over and helped us by writing this new and special book for young people. She has donated all her fees from this book to Medical Aid for Poland.

Helen Exley, Series Editor

North American edition first published in 1990 by
Gareth Stevens Children's Books
RiverCenter Building, Suite 201
1555 North RiverCenter Drive
Milwaukee, Wisconsin 53212, USA

Library of Congress Cataloging-in-Publication Data

Craig, Mary.
    Lech Walesa / by Mary Craig.
       p.   cm. — (People who have helped the world)
    Includes index.
    Summary: Traces the life of the Polish union organizer who was instrumental in gaining government recognition for Solidarity, an organization of local unions, and who won the 1983 Nobel Peace Prize.
    ISBN 1-55532-846-6. — ISBN 1-55532-821-0 (lib. bdg.)
    1. Walesa, Lech, 1943—Juvenile literature. 2. NSZZ "Solidarnosc" (Labor organization)—Biography—Juvenile literature. 3. Trade-unions—Poland—Officials and employees—Biography—Juvenile literature. [1. Walesa, Lech, 1943- . 2. Solidarity (Polish labor organization) 3. Labor unions—Biography.]
    I. Title. II. Series.
HD6735.7.Z55C73   1988
322'.2'0924—dc19   [B]   [92]   88-17732

Series conceived and edited by Helen Exley
Picture research: Diana Briscoe
Editorial: Margaret Montgomery
Editor (US): Rhoda Irene Sherwood
Research editor (US): Mary Jo Baertschy

Printed in Spain

1 2 3 4 5 6 7 8 9 96 95 94 93 92 91 90

LECH WALESA

The leader of Solidarity and campaigner for freedom and human rights in Poland

by **Mary Craig**

Gareth Stevens Children's Books
MILWAUKEE

Nazi occupation

On September 29, 1943, amid the appalling chaos and misery of the Nazi occupation, Lech Walesa was born in the little Polish village of Popowo. In 1939, Nazi Germany and the Soviet Union had carved up Poland between themselves. For Poles a period of unimaginable hardship and persecution had begun.

As the world knows, Germany's leader, Adolf Hitler, hated Jews and wanted to be rid of them. He also despised the Slavs and wanted their lands for Nazi Germany, the German Reich. He urged his henchmen in occupied Poland to kill "all men, women and children of Polish race or language." If the war had continued much longer, they might have done so!

"The Poles will work," said Hans Frank, the governor of occupied Poland. "They will eat little. And in the end they will die. There will never again be a Poland." Everybody who just might emerge as a possible future leader was to be liquidated. Hostages were rounded up and shot by the thousands. Blond and blue-eyed children were kidnapped off the streets and sent to Germany to be brought up as "Aryans" — the so-called pure, untainted "Master Race" of which Hitler and his Nazis dreamed.

When the Germans overran Poland, Lech's father, Bolek, was living with his wife, Feliksa, and their three small children in a two-room stone hut on a small patch of poor, marshy ground. Their part of Poland had been incorporated into the German Reich, and every trace of Polish identity was being removed. Polish places soon had German names. Polish flags, books, and libraries were destroyed; Polish schools were closed down. German colonists took over the Polish lands, while the Polish farmers became farmhands or were sent to work as slaves on the German military fortifications along the rivers.

Opposite: Concentration camps set up in Poland for all who opposed the Reich in any way or who were considered racially inferior were the scene of wholesale slaughter. Many prisoners were killed on arrival, others simply worked to death. Lech's father died as a direct result of his years in a concentration camp. Surrounded by electrified barbed-wire fences and watchtowers manned by heavily armed guards and killer dogs, prisoners had little or no chance of escape, except, as one prison commandant told them, "through the chimmeny." This picture shows Polish prison workers, as depicted by a fellow prisoner.

Below: Nazi guard kicking a prisoner. Reproduced from a picture now in the Dachau Museum, Germany.

Top: Execution of Poles in Ustron, Silesia, 1939. When the ill-equipped Polish army withdrew from Silesia in September, volunteer battalions continued to fight. Volunteers captured by the Germans were immediately shot. Eleven million people were killed in Poland — the country that saw the worst loss of life in World War II.

Opposite, below: Polish youngsters build a road in Germany under strict military surveillance. Many Polish girls and boys were taken from their families, deported, and forced to work in this way. The German policy was to work Polish people until they were no longer of use — and then to exterminate them.

"Poland [became] the home of humanity's holocaust, an archipelago of death factories and camps, the scene of executions, pacifications and exterminations which surpassed anything so far documented in the history of mankind."

Norman Davies, from God's Playground: A History of Poland, *Volume II*

Lech's father arrested

Like most of the Polish peasants, Bolek Walesa supported the Polish resistance movement, the Home Army partisans. Its members hid in the forest by day and came out at night to collect food and to sabotage the German lines of communication. By sheltering and feeding the partisans, the peasants risked their lives, and many of them were indeed shot or strung up from lampposts for this crime.

Lech's sister, Izabela, was nine years old at the time and remembers going into the woods with food and taking blankets to the men who met secretly by night in the Walesas' cowshed. And she remembers with horror that day in September 1943, just before Lech was born, when the men of Popowo were rounded up. Seeing the soldiers, Izabela and her younger brother, Edward, ran into the forest. When they came out again, their father, Bolek, and their uncle, Stanislaw, had been taken away.

Death and a birth

Many of the men arrested in that roundup were beaten to death during the first few days. Though badly beaten about the head, Bolek survived. He was sent

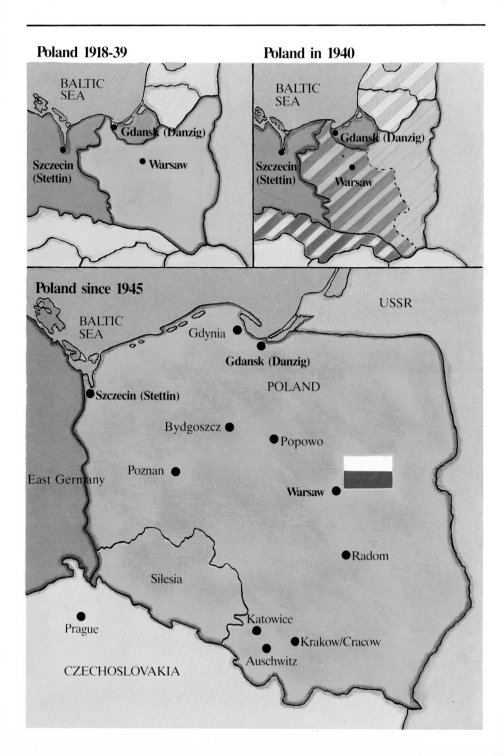

Poland 1918-39

BALTIC
SEA

Gdansk (Danzig)

Szczecin
(Stettin)

● Warsaw

Poland in 1940

BALTIC
SEA

Gdansk (Danzig)

Szczecin
(Stettin)

Warsaw

Poland since 1945

BALTIC
SEA

USSR

Gdynia ●

Gdansk (Danzig)

POLAND

● Szczecin (Stettin)

Bydgoszcz ●

● Popowo

East Germany

Poznan ●

Warsaw

● Radom

Silesia

Prague ●

Katowice ●

● Krakow/Cracow

Auschwitz ●

CZECHOSLOVAKIA

off and forced, under constant threat of death, to work digging trenches and building bridges while his pregnant wife, Feliksa, was left to look after the family farm, their three children, and her expected baby single-handedly.

It was into this unhappy situation that Lech was born. He would never know his father, for in 1945, when the war ended, Bolek struggled home only to die, entrusting Feliksa and the four children to the care of his brother, Stanislaw.

One-fifth of the population of prewar Poland had been killed in the war, and of these almost 90% had been shot, hanged, or gone to their death in the concentration camps. Nor were Poland's fortunes about to improve. When the Germans were expelled, the Soviets of the Red Army moved in. Nazi tyranny was immediately replaced by a Communist regime controlled by Joseph Stalin in Moscow.

In the postwar years, the countries of Eastern Europe — Poland, Hungary, Romania, Bulgaria, and Czechoslovakia — all became part of the new Soviet empire. And although Stalin had once said that imposing communism (with its denial of individual freedom) on the freedom-loving Poles would be like trying to put a saddle on a cow, the cow was, under protest, duly saddled.

The ruthless postwar takeover of Eastern Europe by Stalin marked the start of what soon came to be known as "the Cold War" between the Soviet Union and the West. It resulted in both sides' entering into a disastrous and expensive arms race.

A pauper's childhood

The Walesas were not concerned with politics; their energies were devoted merely to surviving. "We weren't just poor, we were paupers," said one of Lech's brothers. A year after Bolek's death, his brother, Stanislaw, had married Feliksa and they had three children of their own.

So there were two adults and seven children in that tiny cottage with its earthen floor, two rooms, and no electricity. Life was very difficult. Stanislaw didn't have much luck with farming his piece of land and found it hard to make ends meet.

"Almost certainly for political reasons, the world has learned little to this day of Russia's part in the crucifixion of Poland. Yet in the first two years of this, one of the most brutal occupations in human history, the . . . Russians had long experience . . . in the effective application of psychological terror."
Mary Craig, from
The Crystal Spirit

Opposite, top left: Free, independent Poland. After centuries of partial or total occupation, Poland enjoyed independence from 1918 to 1939.

Top right: In 1939, in a secret pact, Stalin and Hitler divided Poland. This 1940 map shows Soviet-occupied Poland in the east and German-occupied Poland in the west.

Bottom: At the end of World War II, Poland was Poland again. But as part of the cynical Yalta agreement, it became part of the Communist-dominated Eastern bloc. For the last forty years, it has been neither free nor independent.

Harvesting in peace, 1945. The war is over at last, the Germans have been driven out by the Red Army, and life returns to a semblance of normality for Poland's largely peasant population. Industrialization has not yet begun. Here, on a farm near the former border with East Prussia, farm workers gather in the first harvest in six years.

"In one sense we had nothing, but you can't judge poverty by material standards. We weren't well-off, we didn't have television, or even radio, but we had books, and the whole world of nature was open for us to read. We were rich in the things that mattered."

Lech Walesa

The family did not exactly starve, but for the most part their diet consisted of only potatoes, milk, and noodles. Buttered bread was a rare treat and very occasionally there was a piece of meat. The children had to tend the geese, take the cows out to graze, weed the fields, sow and harvest hay, and do manual jobs around the house before and after school.

A restless spirit

School was in Chalin, a village about 2.5 miles (4 km) away, to which the children walked, usually barefoot, each morning. Lech was better at sports than at academic subjects, though he did not distinguish himself in either. "I didn't really spring into life until the last bell rang," he says, recalling the way he and his friends would play soccer with a homemade ball or fling themselves into the lake near the school to see who could swim the farthest.

Lech, whose surname — Walesa — means "a restless spirit," lived up to his name. "He used to go off on his own and think about things more than we did," says Izabela. "He was always different, like the cat who walked by himself."

At school he would argue with the teachers a lot and get into trouble. "They taught us communism," he says, "and I didn't pay any attention. Once I was sent to the headmaster and he broke a cane over my head. The trouble was that if I could see that something or other was white, no one was going to persuade me that it was really black."

At home, Lech was frequently at loggerheads with his stepfather, Stanislaw, who was a harsh disciplinarian. Feliksa, a gentler person, had an enormous influence on him. She was a deeply religious woman, cultured and well read, with a lively, inquiring mind and a great interest in history and current affairs. All day long she scrubbed, sewed, and cooked for the family, and gave advice to friends who constantly dropped in to see her. Yet in the evening, she had energy left for reading aloud to her children from the Polish classics.

Thanks to these memories, Lech recalls his childhood as a rich one.

The Polish revolt of 1956

From his earliest years, Lech was aware of "all the wrongs, the degradations and the lost illusions" suffered by the Polish people. So in June 1956, although only twelve years old, he was deeply affected when the Poles — hungry, overworked, badly housed, and oppressed — rose in revolt against the Communist regime. Stalin had died three years earlier, but the repressive system was still in place.

Thousands of workers in the city of Poznan went on strike and took to the streets, calling for "bread and freedom." The Polish government called out troops to quell the riots, and many people were arrested, wounded, or killed.

As a result of this violent protest, there was a great upheaval in the country. A new government was formed under Wladyslaw Gomulka, who was installed as leader of the Polish United Workers' party. Many reforms were promised.

The Polish people called this period their "Springtime in October" and were hopeful that things would now change for the better. They were, alas, doomed to disappointment, since for all but the privileged supporters of the regime, life went on being bleak and hopeless.

Above: two rooms housed the Walesa family of two adults and seven children.

Below: Crosses erected in Poznan in 1981 remind everyone of the workers' uprising in 1956.

The Black Madonna of Czestochowa, symbol to Poles of their national identity. In 1655, Poland was about to fall to an invading Swedish army. The people felt only a miracle could save them. A miracle did. When the Swedes reached Czestochowa, they encountered some last-ditch resistance — a handful of soldiers surrounding the picture of the Virgin. After a futile siege of forty days, the enemy withdrew. Amazed by this extraordinary happening, the nation pulled itself together, expelled the Swedes, and proclaimed that the Blessed Virgin was thereafter to be venerated as "Queen of Poland." More than three hundred years later, she still is!

Trade school

At home in Popowo, Lech Walesa longed to get away from the unrewarding drudgery of farm work. In the late 1950s, Polish peasant boys were deserting their villages in droves, flocking to the shipyards of the newly built and industrialized Baltic Sea towns, like Gdansk and Gdynia. Yearning to follow their example, in 1959 sixteen-year-old Lech enrolled for a three-year course in mechanized agriculture at the trade school in Lipno, Popowo's nearest large town.

Each week he spent three days getting paid, practical experience in a workshop. He spent another three days studying math, metallurgy, technical drawing, physics, and more general subjects such as Polish and history. History, which he thought had little to do with real life, was always his weak spot. The money he earned in the workshop went to paying his hostel fees. Even by Polish standards of those days, Walesa was so poor that both teachers and pupils felt sorry for him.

He was a quiet, hardworking, and determined student. Although an entry in the hostel conduct book complains that "Walesa, Lech: smokes and is a troublemaker," his final report from the trade school assesses his achievement as "fair" and declares him to be "sound in morals and politics."

The director of the school thought him a superb organizer, recalling that when it was Lech's turn to take charge of a weekly work party to sweep out the school corridors, he needed no advice or assistance from any of the teaching staff.

Military service

Leaving trade school in the summer of 1961, when he was almost eighteen, Lech spent two years as a mechanic, mending electrical machinery at a state agricultural depot near home, before being conscripted into the Polish army.

He enjoyed this two-year military service away from the hard work and poverty of home, won the prize for target shooting, and was made a corporal. "I didn't have any trouble from the men," he recalls. "I managed to get further with them through good humor and jokes than others did through shouting at

A Soviet propaganda poster by artist Dimitry Orlov. The poster supports the position of the Communist Red Army and shows a member of the Red Guard stomping on "Polish capitalist oppressors." Across centuries of suffering, Poland has been attacked by Russia to the east and Germany to the west.

them." Lech gave lessons in Morse code and ran courses in electricity and radio navigation. In fact he did so well — and liked the uniform so much — that he considered making the army his career.

But he changed his mind and in 1965 returned home to begin work in another State Agricultural Depot near Popowo. Since Izabela was now married, and Edward and Stanislaw were working away from home, Lech found himself with all the responsibilities of the oldest of the family. He chafed at the limitations of his life.

At work, he was known as "golden hands," because of his skill at repairing everything from a rusty tractor to a television set or a motorcycle. But he could not earn even enough money to buy the secondhand motorbike he wanted. And when his girlfriend, Jadwiga, broke up with him, he came to a crisis point. "I was twenty-four and had achieved nothing of any significance. I felt lonely and empty and somehow I knew in my bones that I was in the wrong place."

A one-way ticket to Gdansk

So one afternoon, without saying anything to anybody, he went down to the railway station and bought a one-way ticket to the Baltic coast.

As a child, he had once been on a school trip to Gdansk, and it had left him with a lingering memory of the sea — "something vast, stretching out endlessly — possibly freedom." Gdansk spelled adventure into the unknown. So it was to Gdansk that he went, to meet his destiny, far from the restraints and traditions of peasant life.

In the great Lenin Shipyard in Gdansk, Lech Walesa found work as a ship's electrician. The shipyard was very different from the rural setting and rusty farm equipment he had left behind, and at first, he found it strange working with a team instead of on his own. But he soon settled down and for the first time in his life had a taste of freedom. By way of a bonus, he would be able to train on the job as an electrical mechanic.

Hardship and disillusionment

But his actual working conditions horrified him. There was hardly any safety equipment, no dressing rooms, no washing facilities, no drying machines. Men who worked outside in all kinds of weather would frequently go home soaked to the skin. Since most of them began work at six in the morning and the only break was from 9 to 9:15, few could get anything to eat or drink until they returned home at three in the afternoon. As a result, many of them suffered from stomach troubles.

Nor were the hostels much better: "A metal bedframe with a lumpy mattress, a floor and four grey walls, all filthy and reeking of mildew, a rickety table and two chairs, each missing at least one leg." A man, said Walesa, could eat and sleep in such a place, but not really live.

Even though most of them realized they were being exploited, they were powerless to do anything about it. The trade unions were official organizations of the Communist party that existed only to make them work faster and produce more and more for the same wage. "Human dignity and the chance to be

"Our shipyard looked like a factory filled with men in filthy rags, unable to wash themselves or urinate in toilets. To get down to the ground floor where the toilets were took at least half an hour; so we just went anywhere. You can't imagine how humiliating those working conditions were."

Lech Walesa

fully responsible for one's own life," Lech said, "were not available options."

Slowly he began to see that whatever changes were made at the top, the workers always lost out. And with that realization came "a deep, irresistible urge to go out and change things." It would not be long before the urge became a passionate, lifelong political commitment.

Student protests

Trouble began in March 1968 with student riots. That year, all over Western Europe, students were making some kind of protest, but by and large it was for more power over their own affairs and an end to the traditional way of doing things.

In nearby Czechoslovakia, the regime of Joseph Stalin had been overthrown and a more liberal leader, Alexander Dubcek, had been installed. Polish students were inspired by this event and began demanding something much more basic: the right to hold and express opinions of their own. They wanted an end to the deadening official censorship that prevented them from saying, reading, or writing anything that met with the regime's disapproval.

In government eyes, such demands were irresponsible. Three thousand students were arrested, hundreds were injured on the streets, hundreds more expelled from their universities with a black mark against their names. This would make it impossible for them to get any but the most unskilled jobs in the future. Thirty thousand were sent into exile.

Meanwhile, the brave attempt to establish "communism with a human face" in Czechoslovakia came to a sorry end when the Soviets and their allies in the Warsaw Pact invaded Prague and restored order by force. To the disgust of most Poles, Polish troops were used in the exercise.

The Soviet leader, Leonid Brezhnev, proclaimed his infamous Brezhnev Doctrine — which stated that whenever a Communist regime was "threatened from within," the Soviet Union and its allies were entitled to intervene with military force.

Though they had disapproved of the use of Polish troops against the Czech rebels, Polish workers hadn't

The Lenin Shipyard in Gdansk employs fifteen thousand people. It builds between twenty and thirty ships weighing 200 thousand tons each year — 70 percent of them for the USSR.

> *"I am a radical but not a suicidal one. I am a man who has to win, because he does not know how to lose. At the same time, if I know that I can't win today because I don't have a good enough hand, I ask for a reshuffling and then check whether I have got a better hand. I never give up. I am a radical, but I don't walk into a stone wall with my eyes shut."*
>
> *Lech Walesa*

cared too much about the fate of their own students. Why should the workers care about the students' lack of freedom when they were hungry and cold?

The authorities tried to stir the workers' indifference into hostility by making them attend public meetings at which students were labeled "spoiled brats" and "hooligans" and blamed for everything going wrong in the country, including the workers' low wages.

Some fell for this line. Lech Walesa was among those who did not. He and a few friends tried to point out that if the students and intellectuals were being persecuted by the government, that was good enough reason for the workers to support them. It was his first plea for social solidarity — and it failed.

Marriage

March 1968, besides marking Lech's first steps into politics, was important for another reason, too. One day, through the window of a flower shop in Gdansk, he caught sight of nineteen-year-old Danuta Golós. He had dated women before, but this one was different. He asked her out and courted her for the next year. Like Lech, Danuta was country-bred and from a large family. Like him, she had dreamed of escape to the big city.

They were married on November 8, 1969. "We were terribly poor," remembers Danuta. "We were hungry, we had all kinds of problems. But life was very good. I could say it was the happiest time of my life, because Lech and I were always together."

"You don't understand. No one wins against us."
Party boss in
Andrzej Wajda's film
Man of Iron

The presence of Soviet tanks on their soil and of the Soviet fleet in the Baltic served to remind the Poles of the ever-present threat of military punishment should they be tempted to step out of line.

Right: Empty shelves tell their own story. Shortages of almost everything — food, candles, soap, toothpaste, detergent, toilet paper, razor blades, shaving cream — meant that people rushed to buy whatever they could, not knowing when it might be available again.

Opposite: Waiting became a way of life in "People's Poland." Women rose before dawn to go to town to be outside the butcher's by six. Then they would wait at another shop for bread, fish, or soap.

Below: Love at first sight for Lech and Danuta Golós. She found him to be "different from other men, both in the way he behaved and in his whole attitude to life."

"Something in us snapped"

Life for the Polish people had been getting worse. Food shortages, price increases, and low wages meant constant struggle. Then, on December 12, 1970, the government announced further drastic increases in the prices of food and fuel — with no increases in wages. It was just two weeks before Christmas, the most important family and religious festival in Poland. Housewives were beginning to plan their festive meals. It was the workers' turn to be angry.

Two days later, one thousand shipyard workers surrounded the Communist party headquarters in Gdansk, demanding that the price increases be withdrawn. No one in authority would talk to the workers, and to the men's fury, they were ordered back to work.

On Tuesday, December 15, the shipyard workers called a strike and twenty-seven-year-old Lech Walesa was elected to the three-man strike committee. With Walesa at their head, three thousand workers stormed the police headquarters, intent on releasing the prisoners held there.

Battles between workers and police erupted in Gdansk. Authorities declared a state of emergency.

On December 16, men arriving for the morning shift reported that the yard was ringed by army units, with tanks blocking the exit roads. By this time, says

Shipyard workers whose lunch was one lonely sausage each. It was the discovery that shipyard workers were hungry and their working conditions intolerable that gave Walesa "a deep irresistible urge to go out and change things."

Lech, "Something in us had snapped. It's hard to imagine how people felt: it was a mixture of despair, desire for revenge and a confused sense of impunity."

No one really believed that the army would attack defenseless workers. But it did. As the workers began to leave the shipyard to join the demonstrations, the firing began. That morning four men were killed.

Feelings were running high. Throughout the coastal region, workers began to put down their tools. Ten thousand workers attacked and set fire to the Communist party building. Officials trying to escape were beaten up by the crowd. All day long, the battle raged and by 6:00 P.M., six people had been killed and three hundred injured.

The December 1970 Massacre

As long as they live, the people of Gdansk and its sister-town, Gdynia, will never forget Wednesday, December 16, and Thursday, December 17, 1970.

In Gdynia, on the morning of the seventeenth, workers were mowed down by machine-gun fire on their way to work. Ferocious battles with the police ensued. Hundreds of people were rounded up and arrested. Those who had been killed were buried in secret in the dark of night so that relatives would not know where to find them.

That night, when Walesa finally went home to Danuta and his baby son, Bogdan, he was for the first time, but certainly not for the last, followed by a secret police "shadow."

The anguish and rage of the Polish people spelled the end of the road for Wladyslaw Gomulka. He was hurriedly replaced as leader of the Polish Workers' party. Chosen to replace him was Edward Gierek.

For years, Walesa continued to feel guilty. He felt that he had failed the workers during those days in December 1970. The subject obsessed him. He brooded on every detail of what had happened and analyzed every mistake, wondering what he might have done differently.

Of one thing he was sure: one day they would be given another chance and when that day came he was determined to be ready.

Gierek's promise

Shortly after Gierek came to power, Lech Walesa was one of three shipyard delegates chosen to meet him. Poland's new leader managed to soothe the angry workers by claiming that since he had been a worker himself, he understood their grievances well.

The meeting ended with his pleading to the workers, "Will you help me?" and the workers shouting back, "Yes, we will."

Walesa shouted as enthusiastically as everyone else. In later years he could have kicked himself for being taken in so easily.

At first, once order had been restored to the country, things did seem to improve. The early seventies were the years of détente, when the relationship between the Soviet bloc and the West was more relaxed.

Edward Gierek began investing heavily in new industry, modernizing much old machinery and importing modern machinery on easy credit terms from the West. The goods produced in the new high-tech factories were to be exported to the West in exchange for the hard currency that Poland needed for the repayment of its debts.

Gierek promised "a little Fiat car for everyone and decent housing for every family." Suddenly, the Poles, who had been starved for so long of luxuries that people in the West took for granted, found themselves able to buy such things as refrigerators, washing machines, transistor radios, and television sets. The other, less fortunate, countries of the Soviet bloc were very envious.

Life for women, whether in town or country and regardless of whether they worked outside the home as well as in, was especially hard. Living conditions were primitive and shortages were chronic. And unlike Western women, the Polish women had no modern devices. Their lives were reduced to the daily grind of waiting outside shops, hunting, bargaining, bartering, housework, and again waiting.

The bubble bursts

Unfortunately, it did not last. The price for Arab oil shot up in 1974. This resulted in recession and inflation for the West, and soon there were few buyers for Polish products. To boost the economy, Gierek was forced to borrow more money from Western banks. He also used up any remaining profit from exports to repay the interest on the loan.

Finally, he could no longer import goods at all. He had to rely on those products the Polish factories could manufacture. Almost immediately the factories

The regime gave priority to state farms and cooperatives and deprived farmers of supplies and technical aid. Most peasants used horses, had no access to tractors, and found it difficult to obtain loans. They still sold their produce on the open market but had little incentive to increase production. Excluded from welfare benefits and harassed by local party officials, they, like their counterparts in the factories, eventually became alienated.

began to run out of spare parts for the machines that kept them going.

The consumer boom ended just as abruptly as it had begun. Waiting in line outside shops for hours to buy even the most basic essentials — such as toilet paper, toothpaste, and household products — became a way of life. And worse yet, all food was in extremely short supply.

As far as the Gdansk shipyard was concerned, Gierek's changes hadn't amounted to much. True, the yard had been modernized, but only with a view to increasing production and not with the health or safety of the workers in mind.

Wages had increased slightly, but working hours were longer than ever, and the work itself was, according to Walesa, "exhausting, inhuman labor that ruins a man's health."

Lech speaks out

To his horror, Lech realized that the shipyard management was gradually getting rid of those who had been active in the December 1970 strike. He himself was always given the worst jobs and was never allowed any kind of promotion.

One day in 1976, he could stand it no longer and decided that, whatever the consequences might be, he must speak out. After all, his fellow workers had chosen him to be their favored candidate in the shipyard union elections.

At an election meeting, he furiously denounced the union as being nothing but a "rubber stamp" for the party and accused Gierek of failing to keep any of his beguiling promises.

At just thirty-two, Lech entered the political arena, said goodbye to all hope of an easy life, and began the work that would result in the Solidarity movement.

The workers applauded, but the authorities were dismayed. A few days later, Walesa was fired from the shipyard. "Why are they doing this to me?" he cried angrily to a friend. "I don't drink, I'm honest, I come to work on time." He appealed against the dismissal, but in vain. Fortunately he found a new job overhauling cars in the transport section of the Zremb Building Company.

"I have always believed that I am the steward of whatever talents I've been given and have to use them to the best effect. I'm an average man . . . with many faults. I wasn't prepared for great tasks, but life put me in this situation and I have had to do what I can with it."
Lech Walesa

23

Mother and children living in a seedy two-room apartment. A third of the population were living at or below the poverty line.

1976 — Food riots

But already, discontent throughout the country was reaching a new boiling point. In June 1976, Gierek announced that the price of food had to go up (70 percent extra on meat, for example) and the rate of wage increases had to slow down.

Workers at the Ursus tractor factory in Warsaw showed what they thought of that. They tore up the tracks of the Paris-Moscow railroad line, which ran through the factory. Then they set up a blockade so that no trains could enter or leave Warsaw.

In the town of Radom, workers attacked the Communist party headquarters and set it on fire, after first removing huge quantities of food and drink that the party elite had been enjoying while the people were almost starving.

The government reacted violently: the police went on the rampage, hitting the workers with truncheons, arresting them whether or not they had actually taken part in the demonstrations, and even killing some. Within a few hours, the prisons were bursting and special courts were set up to hand out sentences based on trumped-up evidence and faked photographs.

Predictably, the workers of Radom and Ursus were condemned as "enemies of society" and "hooligans." All over Poland, workers were asked, as they had been asked in 1968 and again in 1970, to denounce such "troublemakers" to the police.

But in Gdansk, Walesa was beginning to realize that if the workers were to have any hope of survival, they must band together and achieve some kind of solidarity. Under the present system, they were denied the right to express their grievances and even to think for themselves. In Walesa's view, without that freedom to be oneself, human life was scarcely worth living.

The plight of Poland's workers was such, he believed, that they must join to become one united, more powerful voice. But they must act with much forethought and wisdom behind those actions. He believed then, as he would express in 1981, "With strikes, we shall all simply destroy ourselves. We must all stand together. . . . We must . . . behave in such a way that future generations will not curse us."

Standing up for human rights

Others in Poland were reaching the same conclusion at the same time. The Roman Catholic church — to which most Poles belonged — was openly championing the cause of human rights and asking for social reform. So too was the Social Self-Defense Committee, or KOR, an organization made up mainly of disillusioned former Marxist intellectuals. This group was set up to bring both legal aid to workers unjustly punished after the riots and financial aid to their families. The members of KOR collected proof of police brutality and judicial corruption — and made their findings known in a variety of new underground publications.

Gierek was livid and ordered an all-out war on the KOR group. Its members were harassed and fired from their jobs, their apartments ransacked and their belongings seized. They and their supporters were regularly attacked, and some killed, by the police or by "unknown assailants" who were somehow never found or brought to justice.

But KOR refused to be intimidated. They had realized that the authorities' greatest weapon was the fear they could instill in people's hearts. "Once you can rise above the fear," said Jack Kuron, a leading member of KOR, "you are a free human being." KOR members insisted on acting openly, behaving as though they lived in a free society, lecturing and teaching openly, signing the documents they produced — and accepting the consequences.

The public began to show open sympathy for the KOR group — and to learn from its example. At the same time, the Roman Catholic church, which had always regarded Marxist (and even ex-Marxist) intellectuals with the gravest suspicion, gave them support and insisted on their right to express their views freely. One of the most impassioned protectors of these basic human rights was Karol Wojtyla, the cardinal of Cracow, soon to become known throughout the world as Pope John Paul II.

By the late 1970s, the Polish economy was out of control. Poland was almost bankrupt, Western banks had run out of patience, and food supplies were dwindling fast. What food was available was usually of poor quality. There was a high level of illness among the working population.

A call for free trade unions

On April 29, 1978, Lech Walesa was one of a group of dissident workers and intellectuals who formed a

Baltic Committee for Free and Independent Trade Unions. At last he belonged to a group whose aims he admired. Avoiding the ever-watchful police, they met in small groups, always in a different place and at a different time, sometimes on a wild stretch of seashore, sometimes deep inside a forest.

Despite all the difficulties and dangers, the group's magazine, *Coastal Worker*, produced a 1,000-word "Charter of Workers' Rights," signed by sixty-five activists, of whom Walesa was one. It called on workers to throw off their apathy and start looking after their own interests. Only by banding together in independent trade unions could they find the strength to challenge the all-powerful authorities.

The police followed Lech's every move — frequently locking him up for two days at a time and then releasing him, knowing that if they wanted to keep him longer, they had to charge him formally. But this did not stop Walesa from distributing leaflets, posters, and copies of *Coastal Worker* in the streets, on trains, or in buses. He even handed them out from the baby buggy when out walking the baby! At work he talked openly of the need for a workers' organization that would defend basic human rights.

Fired again

Not surprisingly, he was fired again. Though angry fellow employees threatened a strike, Lech, who now had a wife and four children to support, urged them to be cautious. "Don't make trouble," he advised, "you'll only get fired yourselves. We're not strong enough yet. But the time is coming when we shall be stronger than they are, and that's when we shall act."

What saddened Walesa was his friends. Though they resented the system under which they lived, they did not believe anything could ever change it. They apparently felt the hopelessness that Danuta Walesa, Lech's own wife, was at one time to voice: "I don't want my children to have the same sort of life Lech and I have had. I wish they could live in a country that was free, without this awful feeling of helplessness."

Eventually, in May 1979, Walesa found work with Elektromontaz, an engineering firm producing electrical equipment.

When the Polish pope, John Paul II, visited his homeland in 1979, he received a hero's welcome. He raised the morale of the Polish people and gave them a new sense of solidarity. On a visit to the Auschwitz concentration camp, where many of his own compatriots had died, the pope laid a wreath on this memorial to the millions of Jewish victims murdered in the camp.

And the police came too! If, for example, Lech went to repair equipment at a building site, they followed on his heels. They demanded to know what he had been doing, whom he had been talking to, and what matters they had discussed. Possibly it was because of this obvious harassment that Walesa began to win more and more sympathizers to the cause of free trade unions.

The Polish pope

To the amazed delight of his fellow Poles, Cardinal Karol Wojtyla of Cracow became Pope John Paul II in October 1978. When he visited his homeland in June 1979, he was given a rapturous welcome, and millions flocked to see and hear him.

"Be proud of your Polish inheritance. Do not be afraid of difficulties. Be afraid only of indifference and cowardice. From the difficult experience we call Poland, a better future can emerge, but only if you yourselves are honorable, free in spirit and strong in conviction."
Pope John Paul II, June 1979

27

The Poles were overjoyed that a countryman of theirs had been elected pope. They believed that this was their reward for all the years of suffering, and they were far more prepared to listen to their distinguished fellow citizen in Rome than to any of the poker-faced men who were their actual rulers. The pope's visit stiffened Polish morale and imparted a new, heady sense of solidarity, a new desire for a fresh start.

Remembering the December Massacre

Lech was stubbornly determined to be present for the 1979 anniversary of the December Massacre.

His fellow workers kept a round-the-clock watch, and when, on the day before the anniversary, a group of policemen arrived at the factory to remove him by force, they smuggled him out in the trunk of a small

Housing conditions were appalling. Young people waited fifteen years for a three-room apartment in a bleak building, where the bath was usually out of order for lack of spare parts. Often, two or three generations lived together in crowded apartments in difficult circumstances.

car. Lech went into hiding and did not emerge until the evening of December 16, when he joined seven thousand men and women at the shipyard gate in a service of remembrance.

Walesa arrived late. Being at the back of the crowd as well as fairly short, he climbed onto someone's shoulders to make himself heard. It was an improvised speech, but he held the whole crowd spellbound as he spoke of the part he had played in the tragic events of 1970 and of the hopes that Edward Gierek had betrayed.

His words created a powerful bond with his audience, many of whom must have become aware of Lech Walesa for the first time that night. He begged everyone present to organize themselves into groups for their mutual protection. And he ended his address with a stirring appeal: "Next year, on the tenth anniversary, you must bring a handful of stones to this spot. We shall cement them together and build ourselves a monument."

The authorities acted swiftly. The next day fourteen men were fired at Elektromontaz, twelve of them members of the free trade union groups. Lech Walesa, acknowledged as the company's most outstanding electrician, was among them.

Once again he was out of work — with a family of five to support and a sixth child on the way.

Poland sinks into despair

Poland was almost bankrupt. Food supplies had dwindled, and the lines of people waiting outside shops had grown even longer. Women rose before dawn to go into town to be outside the shops by six. If they were lucky, they might get some meat.

Families were living in overcrowded apartments. Young people had to wait fifteen years for a three-room apartment in which the bath was usually out of order for lack of spare parts. Goods produced in Poland found their way to the Soviet Union.

As everything continued to get worse, the government assured the people that everything was going splendidly. Most Poles despised the party, which daily fed them so many lies, and they longed for more honesty and openness.

"Before the war you could see a sign saying BUTCHER and go inside and find meat. Nowadays you see a sign saying MEAT but inside there is only the butcher."
Polish joke

"It was bad enough that there was next to nothing in the shops. But to raise the price of nothing took the people over the top."
Tim Sebastian, correspondent, speaking on BBC-TV, 1980

29

Strike at the shipyard

Lech and Danuta now had four boys and a girl; a sixth child, a girl, would be born in 1980, at almost the same time as Solidarity.

Just as the birth began, the militia came to arrest Lech yet again. Danuta screamed at them to leave him alone. But in vain. Lech returned from his interrogation to find her in the hospital with baby Ania. The humiliation of that night went deep. Lech's anger flamed against a system that had so little regard for the dignity of ordinary human beings.

All over the country in that summer of 1980, minor strikes were breaking out in protest against the food shortages and rising prices.

At the huge Gdansk shipyard, the workers were additionally enraged at the firing of Anna Walentynowicz, just five months before she was due to retire. She was a grandmother who operated a crane and happened to be a dedicated — and popular — champion of workers' rights and free trade unions.

On the morning of August 14, members of "Young Poland" had distributed leaflets asking the workers to come out on strike for the reinstatement of both Mrs. Walentynowicz and Lech Walesa.

Lech climbs over a wall

Lech Walesa went into the shipyard — fully expecting to be arrested on the way — walked around to an unused side entrance, and was hoisted by waiting friends over a perimeter fence. It was one of the decisive moments of Polish history.

The shipyard director was standing on a bulldozer truck, arguing with the men. He had almost persuaded them to go back to work. Suddenly, a small stocky figure appeared on the foot of the bulldozer, which towered over him.

"Remember me," yelled Lech. "I gave ten years' work to this shipyard and then was fired. Well, I'm here to tell you we're not going to listen to any more of your lying promises."

As most of the men knew him at least by reputation, all talk of returning to work was abandoned. Lech called for an immediate sit-down strike, and persuaded the workers to elect a committee

and work out their demands. At this stage, they were simple: the reinstatement of Lech and Anna; immunity for strikers; a small pay raise; and permission to erect a monument forty-four feet (13 m) high for the martyrs of the 1970 massacre.

Showdown

The next day the other shipyards in Gdansk and Gdynia joined the sit-down strike. It was the start of a full-scale showdown with Poland's rulers, unprecedented within the Soviet bloc. From this tiny beginning grew an interfactory solidarity strike which in the end would embrace almost the whole of Poland and expose the hollowness of the regime's claim to represent the Polish people.

August 1980, the Gdansk shipyard. Lech Walesa (seen in the middle of the picture) is the workers' leader during the historic interfactory solidarity strike which eventually changed the face of Poland. Gates festooned with red and white flowers, Polish flags, and pictures of Pope John Paul II separate the sit-in strikers from their supportive families and friends.

An improvised Mass attended by 1,500 workers and their sympathizers on the other side of the gate. The Roman Catholic church had emerged as a powerful champion of human rights in a country where legitimate protest was impossible and where no political opposition was allowed.

*"Give over telling us
  you're sorry,
What guilt for past
  mistakes you carry;
Look in our faces,
  weary slaves,
Gray and exhausted
  like our lives.
"Give over calling us
  the foe
Of all society, of our
  brother;
Just count our numbers,
  and you'll know
How strongly we can
  help each other. . . . "*

*From an unofficial collection
of young strikers' poems
circulated during the
shipyard strike, August 1980*

The original short list of localized demands was soon replaced by a much larger one of twenty-one items. It included a demand for an uncensored press, the right to strike, freedom of belief and expression — and, most of all, the right to free and independent trade unions.

The strike committee's manifesto stated clearly for all to read: "The workers are not fighting merely for a pittance for themselves, but for justice for the entire nation. We must live up to the immortal words, *Man is Born Free.*"

This was not just a strike but an ethical revolution!

The strikers' demands reflected the whole nation's misery over food shortages, poor medical care, long waiting lists, and the disgraceful inequalities that existed between the privileged few and the vast majority of the people. The workers were seeking both a fairer deal and an end to lies and half-truths.

A Solidarity sit-in

As strikers from over five hundred factories joined the shipyard workers, the strike ceased to be a shipyard affair and became a workers' solidarity strike. It grabbed the attention not only of Poland but also of the entire world, and foreign journalists and television crews began to pour into Gdansk.

It was as though the Polish people had awakened from a deep sleep.

Families and friends could talk to the strikers only through the railings by the gates, gaily festooned with pictures of the pope and fresh flowers of red and white, as in the Polish flag. As food was passed in to the workers, a team of women cooked and prepared it in an improvised kitchen. Alcohol, by general consent, was banned, and the ban was strictly observed. Strikers slept where they could: on the grass, cement floors, air mattresses, tabletops, or sheets of polystyrene.

Lech takes charge

Lech was the hero of the hour. Although the strike was led by an interfactory committee and was receiving skilled advice from the intellectuals of KOR, it was the shambling, untidy little electrician with the long mustache who seemed to have his finger on the pulse of the strikers. He looked more like Charlie Chaplin than a hero, but he had a natural authority, an instinctive understanding of the strikers' needs and feelings. Lech spoke a language the strikers could understand, light-years removed from the meaningless official jargon in which they were usually harangued.

When things threatened to get him down, he would draw aside to pray. Prayer, Lech has said, gives him strength. "I fear nothing and nobody, except God." Every evening in the Lenin Shipyard there was Mass, and observers from outside Poland were bewildered. They were unaccustomed to the spectacle of all those thousands of workers on their knees, fervently praying and singing hymns.

"People came from the city by bicycle or on foot; they baked and cooked and carried food and cigarettes. Horse-drawn carts began arriving at the docks laden with potatoes, cabbages, cheese and apples from the farmers. There was even a cartload of pigs. . . . Taxis cruised around, offering transport to anyone bringing food for the strikers."

Lech Walesa

Walesa has never seen himself as anything but a typical Polish worker. "Go down to the shipyards," he has said. "Talk to anyone there. Everyman's story is my story."

The regime gives in

As other industrial cities set up interfactory committees of their own and smaller strikes continued to erupt across the country, the regime panicked, realizing it had lost control of the situation.

What was to be done? With the Soviet government insisting that matters must not be allowed to get out of hand, Edward Gierek was extremely unwilling to negotiate with an independent strike committee that seemed suddenly to be speaking for the entire Polish work force.

He tried sending a minor official to negotiate separately with representatives of each of the factory units, hoping in this way to divide them. But it was too late for that sort of double-dealing, and Gierek was reluctantly forced to send one of his best negotiators, a deputy prime minister for economic affairs, Mieczyslaw Jagielski, to talk with the whole strike committee.

Jagielski and his team arrived in a special bus on the evening of Saturday, August 23, 1980. As the bus reached the yard, a crowd of twenty thousand angry workers surrounded it, shouting "Get out and walk," and "On your knees to the workers." This ugly situation was saved by Walesa's arriving to greet the delegates. With considerable skill, he calmed the men down, persuading them to let the nervous Jagielski pass unharmed through their ranks.

The talks begin

Inside a glass-walled room — with hordes of workers, journalists, observers, and photographers peering through the glass and with every word relayed by loudspeakers to the workers outside — the urbane and well-groomed Jagielski came face to face with Lech Walesa, scruffy as ever.

"These strikes must stop," Jagielski began. "Well, that depends on you," answered the brash little electrician, puffing imperturbably at his pipe. "Where do you stand on our twenty-one demands?"

"Allow me to make a few general points," bluffed Jagielski.

But Walesa was not letting him off the hook. "No, I want a solid answer, point by point."

August 1980, the Gdansk shipyard. With the world watching every move, talks at last take place between the Polish workers and a government team. Every word was relayed by loudspeakers to the crowd waiting outside.

Those listening outside could hardly believe their ears. In Lech Walesa they had a spokesman who could stand up to a party bigwig from Warsaw.

A week later the bargaining was still going on. Jagielski had conceded some ground, but on the question of free trade unions, he would not budge. The Soviets, meanwhile, were threatening to invade Poland if "the leading role of the party" in Polish affairs was in any way undermined. Ignoring this blackmail, the miners of Silesia and the steelworkers of Nowa Huta came out on strike and formed their own interfactory committees.

By then, the strikers in the shipyard were exhausted. They were becoming desperately anxious about what actions the Polish government might take next. No one could be sure that the security forces would not move in and start shooting, just as they had in 1970.

SOLIDARITY!

Walesa did what he could to keep them calm. When tensions threatened to explode, he would start singing Poland's national anthem — "Poland is not yet dead, so long as we are still alive" — completely off-key, in a cracked voice.

"He's a rotten singer, but he can certainly talk," they said.

Yet his growing stature was due not only to his talking skill but to the fact that he used words honestly, as they were meant to be used, in a nation whose ruling party had for so long been dishonest. Walesa, calling a spade a spade in rough, ungrammatical Polish, was offering the moral leadership for which Poland was hungry.

By Saturday, August 30, it was clear that by some miracle an agreement would be reached. That night, the excited workers carried Walesa shoulder-high to the main gate. They were wearing stickers proudly displaying the new SOLIDARNOSC logo. Soon, its English translation, "Solidarity," would be recognized worldwide as the name of the first independent trade union in the Soviet bloc. Nations would watch with curiosity and fascination as the Poles continued to fight for the right to organize unions.

Nationwide support for the strike was almost total. This was no undisciplined, disaffected mob, but an entire people discovering its own solidarity. Many people described the phenomenon, saying "We were together at last." Walesa had his finger on the pulse of the strikers from the start. The chemistry between them was like an electric charge.

The Gdansk Agreement is signed

The Gdansk Agreement was finally signed on Sunday, August 31, 1980. Walesa — though a pugnacious fighter — was delighted when former enemies became reconciled, so with the signing of the Gdansk Agreement, he was jubilant. He saw it as "a success for both sides."

Tossing his prepared speech aside, he spoke from the heart: "We may not have got everything we wanted, but we got the most important, our *independent self-governing trade unions.* That is our guarantee for the future. We have fought for all of you. And now I declare this strike to be over."

The applause in the hall was echoed by the ecstatic cheering outside. Walesa signed the agreement with an oversized plastic pen, a souvenir of the pope's visit. Then he went outside to be hurled into the air again and again by the cheering workers. Grinning, he gave them a two-fisted salute, shaking both fists in the air like a victorious boxer. "Better this way than a long, drawn-out struggle," he said. Then on a more serious note, he added, "But the next stage will be harder, and I'm a bit scared of it."

He was well aware that the Gdansk Agreement was only a beginning and that the pitfalls ahead would be daunting. But the majority were more concerned with the triumph of the present moment. No fears for the future could spoil the general euphoria as workers and politicians stood together singing the national anthem. It was almost unbelievable that such a thing could be happening in a Poland that had been Communist for thirty-five years.

The Gdansk Agreement represented an astonishing backing down by the Polish government. If the promises were actually kept (and that was indeed the $64,000 question), the workers had won for themselves the right to strike, a higher minimum wage, and improved welfare allowances.

Censorship was to be limited to what was strictly necessary for security purposes; the state radio would broadcast Mass to the nation every Sunday. From now on, managers in all state enterprises were to be chosen on the basis of merit — because they were right for the job and not because, however sloppy and inefficient, they could be trusted to put the party's interests first.

Sunday, August 31, 1980: Signing the Gdansk Agreement. The workers' demands were accepted — on paper, at least.

37

Solidarity: the dawn of a new era

Hardly was the ink dry on the paper when word came that Edward Gierek had resigned. For the second time in a decade, a Polish workers' revolt had sent an apparently unshakable Communist leader packing. Gierek was replaced by Stanislaw Kania, a man of relatively moderate views.

Almost overnight, self-governing unions sprouted all over the country, and before very long Solidarity had ten million members. It seemed as though almost the whole nation was behind it. Even party members were deserting by the thousands to join.

"It was the dawn of a new era," wrote Lech Walesa in his autobiography. "We felt that after so many years of living upside down, we were at last beginning to walk the right way up."

Enthusiasm positively sizzled as Solidarity (with help and advice from KOR and other intellectuals) began to draw up plans for the transformation of Poland. People sensed their new freedom. For the first time in thirty-seven years they could speak their mind without fear. These were stirring times.

Unfortunately, it wasn't like that everywhere. In some places, the authorities put every obstruction they could think of in the way of the new unions, refusing to recognize them (even in some instances to speak to them at all) and issuing dire threats about Soviet intervention.

*Polish students took to
plastering posters and
political graffiti on the
walls of Warsaw. It was
one of the only ways they
could register their protest.
The dates on this political
poster show the years of
the workers' main protests.*

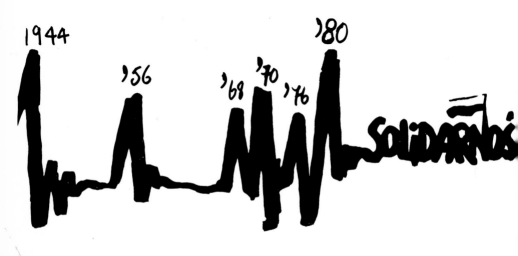

The troubleshooter

Every day hundreds of people went to Solidarity's Warsaw office for advice and support.

It was Lech Walesa they mostly came to see, the unemployed electrician who was now uncrowned king of Poland.

Lech, sprawled in an armchair and wearing an open-necked shirt and jeans, was given no peace. "They brought him their marriage problems, housing problems, everything," said a girl who worked with him at that time. "No one gave him time to think, and everyone expected him to work miracles."

Admiring letters poured in for him, crediting him with every kind of virtue, including sainthood. Admittedly, there was some hate mail and one or two death threats as well.

Lech has never been a modest man, so he enjoyed the fuss and was flattered by the admiration. But he hated having to sit in an office all day long. He had an insatiable passion for journeys and crowds, addressing people all over the country in his crude, slangy Polish, making grammatical mistakes by the ton, contradicting himself constantly, yet holding his audiences spellbound by his enthusiasm and refreshing honesty.

Lech greeted with enthusiasm by his supporters in Warsaw.

"During the sixteen months following August 1980, for the first time in the history of working-class Poland, we were able to take charge of our own problems instead of being helpless dupes . . . in the power struggles of others."

Lech Walesa, from his autobiography, Path of Hope

39

What he called "the Ping-Pong" of questions and answers exhilarated him.

After meetings he was always ravenously hungry but not particularly tired, and an hour's snatched sleep going from one meeting to the next was enough to keep his batteries recharged.

Yet not everyone wanted Lech as leader, now that there was a real possibility of change. His former colleagues on the Free Trades Union Committee asked him to step aside for someone more knowledgeable and competent.

In their eyes, he was simply not up to the job: he was too soft, too ill-informed, not revolutionary enough in his demands. But Lech knew that the workers wanted him and no one else, and he had no intention of stepping down.

"None of us is beyond reproach"

It wasn't easy to lead a movement of such diversity. Now that the August strike was over, many of the workers were eager to settle accounts with those who had made them suffer in the past. They wanted to be rid of incompetent or dishonest factory bosses and government officials who had been feathering their nests for years at the public's expense.

Lech had his work cut out trying to persuade the new Solidarity members that it was foolish to waste their energies on revenge.

Walesa with KOR adviser Bronislaw Geremek. During Solidarity's brief heyday, Lech was in great demand as a speaker all over the country. He showed himself to be a tribune, someone the people could trust to speak for their interests.

And repeatedly Lech also had to assure a nervous government that Solidarity had no political ambitions and no desire to endanger the Warsaw Pact. The pact was the system of defensive alliances with the Soviet Union and the other countries of the Soviet bloc. On the contrary, Solidarity saw its role as that of a necessary permanent loyal opposition. It existed not to challenge the pact but simply to protect the workers' interests.

The regime strikes back

Sadly, Solidarity's moment had come a little too soon, before the people were really ready to cope with the exciting new concepts of freedom and democracy. Lech was well aware that the unions had no clear policies, that they wanted too much too quickly and were inclined to use him as a scapegoat when things didn't go their way.

They needed time to sort themselves out, but time was not available.

The regime cannily exploited this unreadiness to the fullest. The faceless men who ruled Poland and who continued to enjoy the privileges of power had no desire to lose those privileges by keeping the promises they had made in August.

As chairman of the Solidarity National Council, Lech wanted to speak with the authorities, but found he had to fight every inch of the way. It took the threat of a nationwide general strike before he could even get Solidarity officially registered as an independent trade union.

On the day on which Solidarity was finally registered, Lech was the main guest at a triumphant gala of Polish poetry and song at the Warsaw Opera House. His enthusiastic supporters waved banners with legends such as, "Do not be afraid. The whole nation is with you."

But disappointment had already set in, and the workers coped with it in the only way they had found to be effective in the past — they went on strike. Lech soon earned the nickname of "the fireman," because he was kept busy dashing hundreds of miles all over the country, putting out the wildcat strikes that seemed to be erupting all over.

"Are we going to go on forever settling old scores? Our situation is like that wall over there; if anyone takes just one more brick out of it, it'll fall on top of us. The most important thing right now is for us to get together and create a really effective trade union."

Lech Walesa

Lech and Danuta asleep on a bus taking them from one meeting to another. The demands on Lech's time were overpowering, and his private life suffered. Lech was fortunate in that Danuta was a generous and tolerant woman.

The Gdansk monument

On one issue, the authorities had deemed it prudent to give way. The tenth anniversary of the December 1970 massacre saw senior members of the government and armed forces standing in driving, icy sleet with foreign diplomats, bishops, clergy, and 150 thousand ordinary Poles. They were there to unveil the longed-for monument by the entrance to the Gdansk shipyard.

Lech, who always stumbled over a written script, made the clumsiest speech of his life. But it didn't matter. In his eyes the decision to build this memorial was the most important he had ever taken. "Just let them try to knock *that* down," he said, looking proudly at the impressive structure.

But however impressive the ceremony, it represented only a brief truce. The government continued to make promises, then break them again whenever it suited them, and the workers continued to strike as and when they pleased. A new prime minister, General Wojciech Jaruzelski, was brought in — a dour, unsmiling army officer whose eyes were always hidden behind dark glasses.

The stage was already being set for the next act of the drama.

The Gdansk Monument stands just outside the Lenin Shipyard and was the fulfillment of a ten-year dream. The three impressive steel crosses — each of them hung with a black anchor, the traditional symbol of hope and the wartime sign of the Polish Resistance — represent the three abortive workers' rebellions of 1956, 1970, and 1976.

Civil war threatens

Matters came to a head in March 1981 in the small town of Bydgoszcz, where security police broke into a Solidarity meeting and beat up some of its members. There was a huge outcry. Solidarity felt that its very existence was threatened and began to make plans for a general strike.

Even among the Communist party members of Solidarity, support for the proposed strike was widespread. As the countdown began, the air was electric with excitement.

Lech Walesa, however, did not share his colleagues' enthusiasm, since it was obvious to him that the country was about to plunge headlong into civil war. Cardinal Stefan Wyszynski was also very conscious of this danger and gave Lech total support in his attempts to avert it.

Just one hour before zero, Lech's efforts were

Strikes spread across
Poland. The top picture
shows the capital, Warsaw,
paralyzed by a
transportation strike.
At left, a glass factory,
closed by strikers, stands
empty. Lech, with no
national network of offices
and workers, tried to calm
angry groups and did his
best to coordinate the
wildcat strikes.

The family man. Lech and Danuta have eight children, four boys and four girls; two of them, Maria Wiktorja and Brygyda, were born after this photograph was taken. During the Solidarity era and the period of martial law, the six older children, Bogan, Slawek, Przemek, Jarek, Magda, and Ania, knew Lech mainly as an absentee father.

"It was the beginning of the end for Solidarity. It broke our spirit."
A girl in Warsaw

crowned with success, and he managed to reach an agreement with the Polish government.

Delighted to have "defused an enormous charge of dynamite," he presented this agreement to Solidarity's National Commission — a group he had neglected to consult beforehand.

They were furious with him and almost tearing their hair out over what he had done. They believed they had had a chance to bring the authorities to their knees. And Lech had destroyed their hopes.

Some of them never forgave him, and to this day feel bitter about what they see as his high-handedness and betrayal of them.

"I know how far we can go"

Lech, the down-to-earth realist, was unperturbed by the criticism. "I *will* not let things come to civil war," he insisted. "I know how far we can go with our demands. And I know in what country we live, and what our realities are."

He was, of course, alluding to the fact of Poland's inescapable ties to its "Big Brother," the Soviet Union. As the Soviets moved to surround Poland with tanks and warships to the north and east, there were grave fears that they would invade before long.

A travel agency poster in Warsaw suggested wryly: "Visit the Soviet Union before the Soviet Union visits you."

Lech had not been prepared to risk that outcome. But it was the beginning of the end for Solidarity. In his heart, Lech knew that the government was preparing for a war to the death. From now on, Solidarity would be living on borrowed time.

Tragedy

Meanwhile, Lech set off to conquer fresh pastures. His first visit was to the Vatican to meet Pope John Paul II and to talk with Italian trade unionists. After that he went to France, Switzerland, Sweden, and Japan, "to bear witness to our movement before the whole world." Everywhere he went, he spoke of the need for international solidarity among workers.

It was while he was in Japan, on May 13, 1981, that he heard the shocking news of an attempt to

The strain of being Solidarity leader takes its toll. Even in his rare off-duty moments (below), Lech is always surrounded by homegrown and foreign journalists and TV crews. "You've become public property, haven't you?" one journalist asked him. "You mean a slave," he countered wearily. "I haven't got a life anymore. I'm not living at all."

assassinate Pope John Paul II in Rome. In Lech's horrified eyes, the tragedy of the Polish pope was the tragedy of Poland — and of Solidarity.

It seemed as though fate was against the Poles.

Anger and despair

The shops were almost bare now. People slept on the roadside all night so as not to lose their place outside a shop. Potatoes had disappeared completely; meat, sausage, butter, sugar, rice, and flour were strictly rationed and often unobtainable.

Money no longer had any value, and (except in the case of the lucky ones who had access to dollars) bartering took the place of normal buying. There were no cigarettes, matches, or even Poland's national drink, vodka. The factories had run out of spare parts, raw materials, and fuels. Hospital patients could not even be given food — they had to rely on whatever their relatives could scrape together.

As the Poles got hungrier, their anger grew. People were exhausted by the shortages and the endless hours of waiting in lines for the smallest purchase. The government wasn't even pretending to govern, and the country was sliding into chaos. When demonstrations erupted on the streets, the government's only response was to launch a campaign through the media, blaming Solidarity for all the nation's troubles.

At Solidarity's first National Congress in Gdansk in September 1981, nine hundred delegates decided that the time had come to act. Against the advice of Lech Walesa, they called on workers in the Soviet Union and throughout Eastern Europe to form free trade unions.

Lech told them that they were being wildly unrealistic and maintained that the only real way forward was for Solidarity, the church, and the government to get around a table together and discuss a plan of action — as equal partners.

General Jaruzelski takes over

Solidarity's outburst caused dismay among the politicians and in the Soviet Union. One week later, the moderate but ineffective party leader, Stanislaw

By imposing martial law Jaruzelski seemed to the Poles to be declaring war. Their active resistance crushed, the people resorted to quieter methods. Above: a postmark, with its V-for-Victory sign, barbed wire, and black anchor (the symbol of resistance), warned that the Poles did not intend to surrender. Below: a poster calls for Walesa's release from eleven months of solitary confinement.

Kania, was replaced by General Wojciech Jaruzelski. The mysterious general in the dark glasses thus became head of state as well as prime minister and chief of the armed forces.

Although the government did not stop baiting Solidarity through the media, on November 4, 1981, a meeting was arranged between General Jaruzelski, church leader Cardinal Jozef Glemp, and Lech Walesa. When this produced no results, the government stepped up its attacks, probably hoping to goad Solidarity into something foolish.

The beginning of the end came on November 25 when the specially trained riot police, the Motorized Units of Civil Militia, called ZOMO, landed from helicopters to break up a sit-in by students at the Warsaw Fire Academy. Solidarity once again threatened a general strike, and Walesa hastily summoned his executive staff to an emergency meeting in Radom.

The meeting place was bugged. Three days later, Walesa's voice was heard proclaiming on Warsaw Radio that civil war could no longer be avoided. The words he had spoken in that meeting place had been carefully edited; in vain did he protest that he had been quoted out of context and that it was the government that wanted civil war. For the first time, the government-controlled media turned on him personally, calling him "a big liar" and a "provocateur," leader of a group of madmen bent on producing chaos.

On December 11, opening a two-day meeting of Solidarity's National Commission in the Lenin Shipyard where it had all begun, Walesa made a last effort to save the peace. "We do not want confrontation," he insisted.

But Solidarity's commission had had enough and voted the next day for a nationwide general strike, to begin on December 17. They were still arguing when reports began coming in of unusual troop movements, of telephone lines being cut off, of communications with the outside world being severed.

"Now you've got what you've been looking for," Lech shouted angrily, and turning back on them, he went home.

"I do what I have to do, regardless of consequences. Obviously, some people will not like it and may decide to put me behind bars. But it doesn't matter what they decide. The most important freedom is inner freedom, and in that sense I am the freest man in the world. Nobody is free just to act in his own interest; our human freedom is to act within and for the sake of society."

Lech Walesa

The general declares war on the nation

As Saturday, December 12, 1981, drew to a close in a furiously whirling snowstorm, General Jaruzelski struck. All Solidarity buildings were seized. In Gdansk, its leaders were rounded up by the security police. As tanks and riot vehicles rumbled through the streets, the police began arresting Solidarity officials all over Poland.

The dream was over.

Solidarity's five hundred days, which had seen the birth of enthusiasm, excitement, and new hope, were no more. It was game, set, and match to the general.

Early on Sunday morning, General Jaruzelski told a stunned and grieving nation that he had installed a Military Council of National Salvation in order to save Poland from the chaos threatened by "a handful of reckless extremists." The Poles were not impressed. By their reckoning, declaring martial law was declaring war on Poles. Nothing would ever shake their belief in that stark fact, and from then on, they referred to what was happening as "the war."

Martial law

All through that terrible day, a military announcer spelled out what martial law would mean for Poland's people — a curfew from 6:00 P.M. to 6:00 A.M.; all gatherings except for church services banned; no more trade unions or student organizations; no public entertainment or sporting events; no right to strike; no private motoring; and all public transportation to be greatly restricted.

Everybody over age thirty was to carry an identity card and to be prepared to be searched, at home or on the streets, at any moment of the day. Telephone conversations were to be monitored, and travel outside Poland was banned. Military commissars were appointed to all schools and universities.

The arrest of Lech Walesa

In the early hours of Sunday morning, riot police armed with crowbars came to take Lech Walesa away. He was Poland's unofficial leader and famous across the world, but by dawn he was on his way to Warsaw to begin a year-long internment.

Later that day, the authorities tried to persuade him to appear on television to reassure the Polish people that all was well. He refused.

Solidarity had been taken by surprise and had had no time to organize resistance. But in some places the workers did resist, defending their factories and mines against the hated ZOMOs, widely feared for their aggressiveness and ruthlessness.

On December 16, just a year after the impressive monument had been erected in memory of those killed in December 1970, tanks stormed the Lenin Shipyard in Gdansk. People trying to reach the monument that evening met ZOMOs with tear gas and fire hoses.

Similar incidents were reported all over the country, and at the Wujek mine near Katowice, eight miners were killed by the ZOMOs.

But from the villa outside Warsaw where he was interned, Lech Walesa smuggled out an appeal for nonviolent resistance. The Poles were only too glad to respond. Martial law was being carried out with dreadful brutality, and life had become a nightmare.

December 16, 1981. The eleventh anniversary of the 1970 massacre, but in stark contrast to the previous year's ceremonies, ZOMOs broke up the remembrance service with tear gas and fire hoses. In the background is the building where the first shots had been fired by the military in 1970.

49

The six o'clock curfew was violently enforced, and those found out on the streets after that hour were liable to be arrested or even shot. Riot vehicles and tanks were everywhere, and military police seemed permanently to be carrying out identity checks. Telephones were cut off; news broadcasts had once again become a tissue of ridiculous lies.

All those who continued to support Solidarity were fired from their jobs or, in the case of students, expelled from their schools or colleges.

Nonviolent resistance

So the Poles responded to Walesa's appeal for nonviolence in various imaginative ways. They stopped buying the official newspapers or watching television. They would go for walks at television news time, or put their sets in front of their windows, the screens facing outward. They listened (as they had during the Nazi occupation) to sources like Radio Free Europe and the BBC in order to gain a true picture of how things were.

The silence of Lech Walesa

Most of Lech's imprisoned friends and colleagues in Solidarity were being treated as if they were criminals, confined in rat-infested cells, without proper medical care or hygiene.

Lech's fate was, for the time being at least, more bearable, probably because the regime still hoped to use him for its own purposes. Jaruzelski was trying to persuade him to cooperate with the military regime and to abandon his friends. He offered to put him in charge of the new official unions which were to replace Solidarity.

But he underestimated Lech. "I will never bear witness against my friends," he declared. He stood firm, refusing to recognize the new unions and insisting that no agreement was possible with the regime until martial law was lifted and the Solidarity leaders released from prison.

Without his colleagues, he said, he had no right to speak, and so would remain silent. From then on, the silence of Lech Walesa became the main symbol of Polish defiance.

Lech was kept in solitary confinement. During this time, Lech and Danuta's seventh child, a girl, was born, but Lech was refused permission to attend the christening ceremony in Gdansk. It was a blow, but not an unexpected one.

Prison gave him time to think and make plans. It also taught him patience. "If we fail in what we set out to do, then we have to start again," he decided. "Nothing is ever final. Life is all fresh starts."

Police violence

Opposition to martial law was growing, and General Jaruzelski was ruthless in dealing with it. On May 3, 1982, Poland's national day, ZOMO riot squads wearing masks attacked a large crowd of demonstrators with firecrackers, missiles, and tear gas. On the anniversary of the Gdansk Agreement, reports came in from all over the country of police opening fire on the crowds of demonstrators, of people being beaten up, of gas canisters being thrown at groups of women, of schoolchildren being arrested and ill-treated.

According to a poem secretly being circulated, it was as though the government regarded the men in tanks and riot gear as the only honest citizens in Poland, while the rest were nothing but "hooligans" and "scoundrels."

Solidarity was essentially nonviolent. Its supporters' lack of violence was in marked contrast to the ZOMOs' violence. On May 13, 1982, several thousand people commemorated the December 13 crackdown. All traffic came to a halt while pedestrians wearing Solidarity badges stood still with hands lifted in the V-for-Victory salute. The ZOMOs responded aggressively. There were many arrests and heavy casualties. The regime described the people who took part in such peaceful demonstrations as "hooligans," "thugs," and "scoundrels."

The freedom that Solidarity had brought existed no longer. People were constantly being arrested and beaten up, including schoolchildren. Yet the Poles remained true to Solidarity's belief in nonviolence. There were no bombs. There was no sabotage. To the Poles, pursuing nonviolent solutions to the nation's problems was a deep commitment.

Toward the end of that terrible year of 1981, General Jaruzelski had declared Solidarity illegal, and therefore nonexistent. Solidarity was, in fact, still very much alive as an underground organization, led by a handful of members who had escaped the roundup of the leaders.

Perhaps to strengthen the impression that Solidarity didn't count any more, Lech Walesa was released from prison. He was a man of no importance, the authorities said scornfully; he was plain Citizen Walesa.

"It is hard to think of any previous revolution in which . . . moral goals have played such a large part. . . . Moreover, it is [a] . . . fact that in sixteen months this revolution killed nobody. . . . This extraordinary record of non-violence, this majestic self-restraint in the face of many provocations, distinguishes the Polish revolution from previous revolutions."
    Timothy Garton Ash, from
    The Polish Revolution:
    Solidarity

Walesa comes home

The Poles thought differently. When their hero arrived home from internment the night of November 15, 1982, a crowd of several thousand waited near his apartment block in Gdansk. WELCOME HOME was painted in huge white letters on the roadside, and banners printed with WE WANT LECH streamed from every window.

November 1982. Lech is released from internment and comes home to Gdansk and his family.

"We had, during those 500 days, set in motion an alternative society, while the whole of Poland awakened from its long slumber. We were not the master of our own house; it was and is still ours, but we had returned to the pauper's role, while others in authority again took over. The people had tasted freedom, and now we had to bide our time."

Lech Walesa, from his autobiography, Path of Hope

They shouted for him and refused to let him go. That night he came to the window nineteen times, shouting encouragement to the crowd below, promising, until his voice finally gave out, that he would never betray them.

From now on, he would be closely watched. In fact, he would never again be able to go out without a police escort.

His apartment was bugged and everything he said or did was reported to the authorities. "My telephone and my walls are all ears," he would warn visitors, adding with a laugh, "I am the freest man in the world. If you're free inside yourself, you're free no matter what the authorities decide to do."

Early on December 16, when he was to speak at the monument to the victims of the December Massacre, six military policemen burst into his apartment, stole him away, and drove him around for eight hours so he would not give his speech.

But Lech had released his speech in advance to Western journalists. That night, at the monument, his words were read aloud in his absence. "We have been hurt once again," he had written. "But our cause is still alive, and victory will one day be ours."

Back to the shipyard

Perhaps it was to keep Lech from causing trouble that in April 1983 he was given his old job at the shipyard again. The man who had been the most important person in Poland, whose face had been known to the entire world, was back to being a ship's electrician. It says a lot for his courage and his character that he took it in stride.

His timetable was exhausting. Up at five to go to work, he would find four security policemen waiting outside the apartment block. Sometimes, if they had fallen asleep at the wheel, Lech would rap on the car's roof and shout, "Wake up. Time to get going!"

One icy winter morning, he even persuaded them to help him get his car started! After work, there were interviews with the foreign press and meetings with Solidarity advisers. When he reached home at around midnight, there were more people to see and hundreds of letters from supporters to answer.

Meeting with Pope John Paul II

Two months after Lech returned to work, Pope John Paul II paid a second visit to Poland and asked to see Lech. The authorities didn't want to give such prominence to "this former leader of a former union." For the duration of the pope's visit, the authorities kept a close watch on Lech and didn't allow him any days off work.

But the pope insisted, and eventually the two men met for two-and-a-half hours. After the meeting, Lech said, "I felt as though I had received an electric charge . . . as though he had passed some of his own peace to me."

In the country at large, things had gone from bad to worse. Food, clothing, and medical supplies were so scarce that truckloads of emergency supplies were being sent in to Poland almost every day from voluntary organizations in the West, to be distributed by the church authorities.

Hospitals were so overcrowded that children slept in corridors or sat on the floor waiting for vacant beds.

Reinstated in his job as an electrician, the man who had been the "uncrowned king of Poland," admired all over the world, was happy to revert to being an ordinary worker and family man.

"I have always been an ordinary worker. . . . That doesn't mean that I have no ambition to improve myself. But to the end of my days I shall be a working man. And why? Because, in my kind of work, I repair tools of old and new, from East and West, from simple hammers to highly complex machines. Now there's a job to expand a man's mind."

Lech Walesa

Lech did not go to Norway to collect his Nobel Peace Prize. He was afraid he would not be allowed back if he left the country. So Danuta and his eldest son, Bogdan, attended on his behalf.

Doctors and nurses lugged laundry baskets up and down stairs, nurses washed soiled sheets and clothing in basins, and orderlies mopped the wards without detergents or disinfectants. Surgeons had to wash disposable articles over again.

The Nobel Peace Prize

One day in 1983, a friend excitedly telephoned Lech at two in the morning to tell him he had won the Nobel Prize for Peace. Lech refused to believe it, and went back to sleep.

Later, he drove off with a group of friends for a day's mushroom picking in the woods of Kashubia, the nearby Polish lake district. His little white car was followed by at least eight taxis full of foreign journalists who had already heard the rumors.

At 11 o'clock, everyone piled out of the cars to huddle over a short-wave radio set. When a German station announced that the Nobel Peace Prize had been awarded to Walesa, his friends grabbed his arms and legs and tossed him into the air several times in triumph. Then they all turned around and went home to find an excited crowd — and hordes of foreign news teams — waiting for Lech.

In his Nobel acceptance speech, read by Danuta, Lech claimed that the award was not for himself but for the achievements of Solidarity, which had remained nonviolent in spite of ruthless violence used against it.

All his life, he said, he had been surrounded by "violence, hatred, and lies" and, finally, the lesson this had taught him was that "we can effectively oppose violence only if we do not resort to it." The Polish people wanted dialogue, not confrontation, with their government.

The end of martial law — and of Solidarity

Unfortunately, it was a message lost on the Polish government. Martial law — which the Poles continued to call "the war" — had officially ended in July 1983. But nothing much had changed, and the government and people were growing farther and farther apart.

Walesa's Nobel Prize had focused the world's attention once again on Poland but had little visible effect on the Polish rulers. They continued their repression while insisting that Lech Walesa was a citizen of no importance whatsoever. The world had recognized Walesa, but his own government was bent on snuffing out the candle of peace that he had lit.

The years of repression

For five years, Poland remained in darkness, still waiting for that brave candle to be lit again. Visitors to Poland described a nation of demoralized "no-hopers," in which the only antidote to endless humiliation and despair was to get out. Outside help from the West was still necessary for survival, and the division between "us" (the people) and "them" (the government) was complete. Many Poles, especially the young, were still immigrating to the West.

Any opposition was met with imprisonment without trial — or even murder. Father Jerzy Popieluszko, murdered in 1984, and Father Stanislaw Suchowolec, murdered in 1989, were just two publicized examples of the fate of the bravest people.

The scene changes

By 1988, the regime was in a state of total paralysis. Wage increases could not keep pace with skyrocketing prices, and the government began to fear a campaign of massive civil disobedience. Discontent boiled over in April and then in August when strikes broke out in Gdansk and other key industrial areas.

Walesa calmed the strikers and appealed again for the recognition of Solidarity. As confidence in the government reached an all-time low, his own prestige grew both at home and abroad. When he was allowed to argue Solidarity's case on television with the head of the party-approved trade unions, he ran rings around his opponent.

The situation became increasingly untenable for the government, which finally turned for help to the "man of no importance." After stormy meetings with his Central Committee, Jaruzelski summoned a round-table conference. There, an impassioned Walesa voiced the discontent of the Poles.

Jerzy Popieluszko, a pro-Solidarity priest, articulated the hopes and fears of the people during martial law. The secret police murdered him in October 1984, causing worldwide outrage. There were other victims too. The Polish Helsinki Committee, which monitored human rights violations, presented a horrifying list of kidnappings, beatings, torture, and murder.

New challenges for Solidarity

Bargaining was bitter and dragged on for weeks, but in the end, the two sides reached a compromise. Solidarity was made legal and a new parliament was established that allowed the election of those who were not approved by the Communist party. Solidarity made concessions, of course. Their group must remain a minority; and the office of president must go to a party nominee.

June 1989 saw the first elections under this agreement. Of 360 seats in the lower house, Solidarity — as part of the negotiations — agreed to run for only 161. They won all 161. The 100-member Senate, newly restored to power, went to

"It's a bit like learning to do the long jump. First a little jump, then a little bit further. We thought we could do more than we were capable of doing, and we were beaten back. But we'll try again. You must have hope."

Lech Walesa

Solidarity members, who won 99 seats. It was a satisfying election — Solidarity had the people's support. When Jaruzelski decided to run for president, he sought Solidarity's help; then he asked that Solidarity form a coalition government with the party. So today Solidarity faces new challenges. Now serving in government, the group must decide exactly how its members will work with the Communist party to solve Poland's economic and social problems.

While today full democracy remains a dream, Poland's people are heartened by the election. They continue to support Walesa and other Solidarity members, deeply grateful for their courage and the sacrifices they have made on behalf of all Poles.

"Lech Walesa has made humanity bigger and more inviolable. His two-edged good fortune is that he has won a victory which is not of this, our political, world. The presentation of the Peace Prize to him today is a homage to the power of victory which abides in one person's belief, in his courage to follow his call."

Egil Aarvik, Chairman of the Norwegian Nobel Committee

For More Information . . .

Organizations

There are countless unions throughout the world representing every group from steelworkers to graphic artists to teachers to shoecutters to steamfitters to people who work for the government. To find out more about local chapters of these unions, check the yellow pages of your telephone directory under "Unions" or "Labor Organizations." Contact local chapters and see if they will provide speakers who will come to your school and do a presentation for your class. You might want to prepare a list of questions ahead of time so that you can ask the representative specific questions.

Listed below are just some of those unions as well as a selection of groups specifically interested in the problems of workers in Poland. Write to these organizations if you want to learn more about labor and government in Poland, about the Solidarity movement, and about conditions for workers in the United States and the world. Some of these groups may have publications that you could subscribe to. When you write, be sure to tell them exactly what you want to know, and include your name, address, and age. If you write to the two European organizations listed below, call your post office to see how much postage your letter will need. Although their offices are in Europe, someone will write back to you in English.

Coalition of Labor Union Women
15 Union Square, West
New York, NY 10003

Committee in Support of Solidarity
275 Seventh Avenue, 25th Floor
New York, NY 10001

Education Department
International Confederation of Free Trade Unions
37-41, rue Montagne aux Herbes Potageres
B-1000 Brussels, Belgium

International Labor Organization
4, rue des Morillons
CH-1211 Geneva 22, Switzerland

Friends of Solidarity
c/o Chris Michejda
21 Frasta Court
Rockville, MD 20850

Solidarity International
c/o Solidarity Support Committee of Rhode Island
340 Lockwood Street
Providence, RI 02907

Books

The books listed below will help you learn more about Poland, about labor unions in the United States, and about well-known people in labor union history. Check your library or bookstore to see if they have them or if someone there will order them for you.

Heroes of American Labor. Morgen (Fleet Press)
The Long Struggle: The Story of American Labor. Haskins (Westminster/John Knox)
Modern Trade Unionism. Flagler (Lerner Publications)
Poland. Greene (Childrens Press)
Poland. Sandak (Franklin Watts)
Poland: Land of Freedom Fighters. Pfeiffer (Dillon Press)
Stolen Years. Zyskind (Lerner Publications)
Take a Trip to Poland. Lye (Franklin Watts)
The Unions. Fisher (Holiday House)
We Live in Poland. Donica and Sharman (Franklin Watts)
The Worker in America. Claypool (Franklin Watts)

Magazines

The following magazines will give you more information about particular careers and about events around the world that affect the lives of working people. Check your library to see if they have them, or write to the addresses listed below to get information about subscribing. Almost every day our newspapers report on events occurring in Poland, so check your daily newspaper or read a major paper in your local library if you are interested in the most recent actions of Solidarity and the Polish government.

Career World
General Learning Corporation
60 Revere Drive
Northbrook, IL 60062-1563

Choices
P.O. Box 644
Lyndhurst, NJ 07071-9985

Current Events
Field Publications
4343 Equity Drive
Columbus, OH 43228

Faces
20 Grove Street
Peterborough, NH 03458

Junior Scholastic (in the United States)
P.O. Box 644
Lyndhurst, NJ 07071-9985

Junior Scholastic (in Canada)
Scholastic-TAB Publications, Ltd.
Richmond Hill, Ontario
Canada   L4C 3G5

U*S* KIDS
P.O. Box 8957
Boulder, CO 80322

Glossary

Aryans
   Originally the name given to all descendants of a group of people called Indo-Europeans. Historians and scholars of language suggest that the Indo-European race was the one from which most West European cultures and languages came. Adolf Hitler narrowed the term *Aryan* so that it came to mean people with "Nordic" features (blond hair and blue eyes) — members of his "master race."

BBC
   The British Broadcasting Corporation, the government-chartered broadcasting network in the United Kingdom which provides some publicly and some privately funded programs.

bloc
   A group of people, parties, or nations united by a common interest.

cold war
   A state of political tension that exists between countries, in particular the USSR and the United States. One aim of a cold war is to gain political and economic advantage without actually fighting. Another is to influence nonaligned countries, countries that are not committed to either side.

communism
   The belief that all people — not just the rich and middle class — should own the resources used to produce goods. According to communist theory, the people should also decide how the goods will be distributed among the people. In a communist system there would be no upper class, middle class, and lower class. People would work at what their talents and energies allowed, and they would receive according to what they needed. Communism is based on the work of nineteenth-century philosopher Karl Marx. He believed that the wealth of a nation would never be distributed equally until there was a government made up of members of the working class rather than people who represent capitalists. He did not realize how persuasive unions might one day be in organizing for the rights of workers.

conscription
   The system under which all able-bodied men (and in some countries, women) are legally required to serve with the armed forces.

détente
   A period when tensions between countries are lessened.

dissident
Someone who does not agree with the official government policy. In the Soviet bloc, dissidents are those who try to persuade their government to take a more democratic and humanitarian approach to the nation's problems. To avoid being silenced by the government, dissident groups often have to circulate their written material secretly.

hard currency
A currency which, because it is constantly in demand and widely accepted, is not likely to suddenly change in value. The U.S. dollar and pound sterling are examples.

Hitler, Adolf
(1889-1945) Born in Austria, he became leader of the Nazi party in Germany. While in prison after an attempted coup, he wrote *Mein Kampf,* expressing his ideas of "Aryan" superiority and his hatred of the Jews and other minority peoples. He became Germany's dictator in 1934. By ordering the invasion of Poland in 1939, he started World War II. Rather than face capture, he killed himself in April 1945, when Berlin fell to the Soviets.

Holocaust
The term applied to Hitler's effort during World War II to exterminate all the Jews and members of other minorities of Europe. The word more generally means a great destruction or loss of life.

KOR (*Komitet Obrony Robotników*)
The Social Self-Defense Committee, set up in 1976 by a group of intellectuals who were formerly Marxists. It provided legal and financial aid to workers who were unjustly punished by the police.

liquidate
To kill a person or persons or to arrange for them to be killed.

loggerheads
Loggerhead refers to many different things: a marine turtle, an iron tool that is heated and used to melt tar or warm liquids, and the post on a whaleboat that secures the rope holding a harpooned whale. The expression *at loggerheads* refers to an open dispute or ongoing quarrel between people or groups.

logo
Abbreviated word for *logotype*, the symbol that an organization or publication adopts to represent itself.

manifesto
A public statement outlining the beliefs, policies, and goals of an organization, usually a political organization.

Marxist
Someone who follows the ideas of two German philosophers, Karl Marx and Friedrich Engels. The term loosely describes any militant communist.

master race
See **Aryans**.

Morse code

An international system of communication invented by Samuel Morse. Patterns of short and long signals, often called dots and dashes, are tapped out to represent numbers and the letters of the alphabet.

Nazi

A member of the National Socialist German Workers' party, which came to power in 1933 under the dictatorship of Adolf Hitler. With a lowercase "n," the word *nazi* also refers to someone who adheres to the policies or beliefs of Nazism. Some beliefs of the Nazis are that the government should control the economy, that the so-called "Aryan race" is superior to other races, and that a nation may invade and dominate other nations. (*See also* **Aryans**.)

Nobel Prizes

Sweden's much-respected annual prizes, awarded for outstanding world achievements in chemistry, physics, medicine, literature, and peace. A sixth prize for economics was first awarded in 1969.

partisan

A member of an armed group that, during wars, operates in territories that are controlled by enemy invaders; also refers to a militant supporter of a belief, a cause, a party, or a faction.

pauper

Someone who is extremely poor. This word also refers to someone who depends upon public charity.

Polish United Workers' party

The ruling communist party in Poland, formed after Poland was declared a "people's republic" in 1947. In Poland, it is usually referred to simply as the party.

Red Army

The former name for the army of the Soviet Union. It was renamed the Soviet Army in 1946.

regime

A system of government; also refers to a government that is in power, as well as a social pattern or social system.

Reich

The name given to the government or territory of a German empire. Adolf Hitler's Nazi regime from 1933-45 was called the Third Reich.

republic

A form of government usually headed by a president. Power lies in the people, who vote for their representatives. Also refers to a group of people working in the same field or sphere who are equals.

Solidarity

The name of the independent trade union set up in Poland in 1980 under the leadership of Lech Walesa. It was formed after a series of strikes in the Baltic shipyards forced the authorities to allow trade unions that were independent of Communist party control to exist.

Soviet Union

Another name for the Union of Soviet Socialist Republics, or USSR, which is made up of fifteen units called republics. The largest of these is the Russian Soviet Federated Socialist Republic, known as Russia.

Stalin, Joseph

(1879-1953) A Russian leader who became the virtual ruler of the Soviet Union by ordering the murder of all opponents in a series of purges in the 1930s. One affair still investigated is the murder of hundreds of Polish military personnel in a Polish forest. For years, the world attributed these deaths to the Nazis, but now Stalin's role in the massacre seems clear. During his rule Stalin transferred industry and agriculture from private to government ownership and liquidated the *kulaks*, peasant landowners who opposed this policy.

tyranny

A government in which one leader has complete power; also refers to complete power that is cruel or unjust.

Warsaw Pact

An agreement for military alliance signed in Warsaw in 1955 by Albania, Bulgaria, Czechoslovakia, East Germany, Hungary, Poland, Romania, and the USSR. Albania withdrew from the pact in 1968 as a result of differences with the Soviets.

ZOMO (*Zmotoryzowane Oddzialy Milicji Obywatelskiej*)

Motorized Units of Civil Militia; made up of 25,000 to 30,000 men. The riot police used in Poland to dog the steps of Solidarity members and their families.

Chronology

1918	After centuries of repeated occupations by Russia and Germany, Poland is revived as an independent republic.
1939	**September 1** — Germany invades Poland. World War II begins. **September 3** — Britain and France declare war on Germany. **September 17** — The Soviet Union invades Poland.
1943	**September** — Lech's father is taken prisoner and sent to a labor camp by the Germans. **September 29** — Lech Walesa is born in Popowo, Poland.
1944	The German army is driven out of Poland by Soviet forces. Poland is under Soviet domination.
1945	**March** — Lech's father is freed. **May** — Lech's father dies. **July** — Poland's boundaries are redrawn at the Potsdam Conference, which includes the leaders of the United States, Great Britain, and the USSR.

1947   Poland is declared a communist people's republic.

1948   The Polish United Workers' party is formed.

1956   The Poznan food riots. Wladyslaw Gomulka is installed as leader of the Polish United Workers' party.

1959   Lech, aged 16, starts a three-year course at the trade school in Lipno.

1963   Lech is conscripted into the Polish army for two years' military service.

1967   **May** — Lech, aged 23, begins work in the Lenin Shipyard in Gdansk.

1968   **March** — Student riots are suppressed by the authorities. Thirty thousand students are sent into exile.

1969   **November 8** — Lech Walesa, aged 26, marries Danuta Golós.

1970   **December 12** — The government announces drastic increases in the price of food and fuel and then declares a state of emergency after violence and strikes break out in the Baltic towns of Gdansk and Gdynia. Edward Gierek replaces Wladyslaw Gomulka as leader of the Polish United Workers' party.

1976   **February** — Lech loses his job at the shipyard after speaking out against the Polish authorities.
Gierek announces further increases in the price of food. Violence breaks out in Ursus and Radom. KOR is set up.

1978   **April 29** — The Baltic Committee for Free and Independent Trade Unions is set up by Lech and other dissident workers.
October — Cardinal Karol Wojtyla of Cracow becomes Pope John Paul II.

1979   **June** — Pope John Paul II visits Poland.
December 16 — Seven thousand people gather at the shipyard in Gdansk to remember those killed in 1970. Lech calls on them to set up independent groups to protect themselves.

1980   **August** — Lech calls for an immediate sit-down strike at the Lenin Shipyard in Gdansk.
August 23 — Lech has talks with Deputy Prime Minister Jagielski.
August 31 — The Gdansk Agreement is signed. Independent trade unions are now allowed to exist.
September — Stanislaw Kania replaces Edward Gierek as party leader.
November — Solidarity is registered as an independent trade union, the first in a Soviet-controlled country.

1981   **January** — Lech meets Pope John Paul II in Rome.
March — Security police beat up Solidarity members during a meeting in Bydgoszcz.
May-June — Lech visits Japan, Switzerland, and France.
September — Solidarity holds first National Congress.
October — Stanislaw Kania resigns as party leader and is replaced by General Wojciech Jaruzelski.

November 4 — Lech meets General Jaruzelski and Cardinal Glemp for talks.
November 25 — ZOMO riot police break up a student sit-in at Warsaw.
December 12 — Solidarity leaders are rounded up.
December 13 — General Jaruzelski imposes a state of martial law and declares Solidarity illegal. Lech begins a year-long internment.

1982 **May 3** — ZOMO riot squads attack a crowd of demonstrators and arrest over one thousand.
August 31 — Second anniversary of the Gdansk Agreement. Trouble flares up all over the country.
November — Lech is released from internment.

1983 **April** — Lech returns to work at the Lenin Shipyard.
June — Lech meets Pope John Paul II during his second visit to Poland.
December — Lech Walesa is awarded the Nobel Peace Prize.

1984 **October** — Father Jerzy Popieluszko is murdered by the security forces.

1986 **July** — The authorities announce a general amnesty. Twenty thousand detainees are released.

1987 **June** — Pope John Paul II's third visit to Poland.

1989 **January** — Two pro-Solidarity priests, Father Stanislaw Suchowolec and Father Stefan Niedzielak, are found dead.
February 6 — Lech opens talks in Warsaw between the Polish government and Solidarity.
April 17 — Solidarity is legalized.
June — Solidarity wins 99 out of 100 Senate seats. Allowed to run for only 161 of the 360 seats in the lower house, Solidarity wins all 161.
July — General Jaruzelski is elected president and asks Solidarity to form a coalition government with the party.
August 24 — Poland's parliament elects Solidarity activist Tadeusz Mazowiecki prime minister. He is the Eastern bloc's first non-Communist prime minister in over 40 years.

Index